Mind Over Spirit

Unmasking the True Enemy of Christian Unity

Samuel Obadare

First paperback edition April 2026

ISBN: 979-8-218-94934-1 (paperback)

www.PasSamBooks.com

Table of Contents

Table of Contents

The Hidden Saboteur

Why Disunity Is the Church's Most Underrated Enemy

What comes to mind when you think of the most potent forces militating against and impacting the church of Christ today? It's most likely that on your list are contenders such as Satan, demons, Islam, social influences, and even new and ever-evolving threats to Christianity in our world today. But what if one of the most potent saboteurs of the church is absent from that list of famous contenders and typically misses the list of what most consider the enemies of the church? Could there be a serious and deadly enemy that the body of Christ is unintentionally closing her eyes to? And if that's the case, what might it be? Well, there is, and that inconspicuous "enemy" is what this book is written to identify, spotlight, diagnose, and proffer a solution to.

Actually, there are several little-known saboteurs that have continued to quietly undermine and debilitate the church's power and potency, chiefly because they have rarely been considered significant or consequential. Near the top of that list is the seemingly innocuous thing called disunity. Disunity is one of the most subtle but potent enemies the body of Christ will ever have. It is so serious and strategic an enemy that even Satan, the church's fiercest enemy—second only to sin—is significantly weakened in penetrating and attacking without it. On the flip side, disunity is such a catalyst that the slightest hint of its presence is like a shark smelling blood in the water. Once the adversary perceives it, he gains both the impetus and the ground he needs to carry out his attacks against the church.

Like a crowbar, disunity is the devil's favorite tool to pry open the door before penetrating and launching his assaults on any community or group. Whether targeting the smallest unit of society – the family, a small group, a Christian ministry, a local church, or the body of Christ at large, disunity remains the favorite and highly effective launchpad for Satan and his minions to launch their schemes and agendas. Like many other believers, perhaps you, the reader, haven't previously considered disunity as an enemy of such magnitude. But it is. It's both pernicious and potent. While we, the body of Christ, mostly focus on and direct our offensives at Satan and his demons, we tend to overlook this insidious enemy, which must neither be ignored nor indulged. On the contrary, disunity is a foe that the church must preempt and proactively combat because it is a strategic enemy that catalyzes and advances other vices against the body. This is why the subject of unity is a major one in the Scripture, with our Lord Himself speaking more about it than anyone else. It goes without saying that if the Lord gives this issue so much weight, the body of Christ should also give it its utmost attention.

It is my hope that this book will effectively expound on the dynamics behind disunity in the family, society, and in the body of Christ – the church, with the view not only to heightening awareness of this enemy but also mitigating it. Welcome aboard as we undertake this important journey together.

The Indispensable Unity

Four Reasons Unity is not Optional for the Church

There are at least four reasons unity is essential for the body of Christ, and why disunity is adversely consequential for her.

Unity in the Divine DNA

Firstly, unity has to do with the nature of God Himself. God exists in a unified state – the perfect, unbroken harmony of God the Father, God the Son, and God the Holy Spirit. This reality implies that disunity is, by its nature, antithetic to the divine nature, and that makes it inimical to the church.

The perfect unity of the Godhead is unmistakably evident right from the creation of the universe, especially in the creation of humanity. Firstly, God reveals Himself in the creation account as Elohim, a masculine plural word in Hebrew: "In the beginning, God [Elohim] created the heavens and the earth" (Gen. 1:1 NKJV). Secondly, when creating man, God uses the first person common plural pronoun "Us": God (the Father) said, "Let Us make man in Our own image according to Our own likeness; let them have dominion over the fish of the sea, over the birds of the air, and over the cattle, over all the earth and over every creeping thing that creeps on the earth" (Gen. 1:26 NKJV). Notice the plural pronouns, "Us" and "Our", which are not a reference to angels or other heavenly beings in conference with God the Father, but rather to the Son and the Holy Spirit.

The plurality of God's name, Elohim, and of the pronouns in the opening pages of the Bible clearly introduces us to the trinitarian nature of God. However, the Bible dutifully makes it clear that there is only one God: "Hear, O Israel: The LORD our God, the LORD is one!" (Deut. 6:4 NKJV). Our Lord Jesus Himself reiterates this same scripture: "Jesus answered him, 'The first of all the commandments is: Hear, O Israel, the LORD our God, the LORD is one. And you shall love the LORD your God with all your heart, with all your soul, with all your mind, and with all your strength'" (Mark 12:29-30 NKJV). The meaning of these two attributes of God – plurality and singularity – is clear: God is One in three Persons. God is Trinity in unity.

Jesus again highlights the unity of the Trinity in the Great Commission: "Go therefore and make disciples of all the nations, baptizing them in the name of the Father and of the Son and of the Holy Spirit" (Matt. 28:19 NKJV). Notice it is, "...in the name," not "...in the names". Apostle John, also emphasizing the unity of the Trinity, writes, "For there are three that bear witness in heaven: the Father, the Word, and the Holy Spirit; and these three are one" (1 John 5:7 NKJV). Clearly, unity is intrinsic and integral to God's Own nature. That makes disunity injurious to the church as it is patently incongruous with God's nature. It is foreign to Who God is. This is the first reason unity is critical for the church: it aligns her with the nature of God Himself.

The Conduit of Blessing

While the spiritual assets and largesses from God have already been bestowed abundantly upon the body of Christ (Eph. 1:3 NKJV), the maximum impact and dissemination of those blessings are only possible through unity and harmony within the body. In his letter to the Ephesian church, Apostle Paul writes, "From whom the whole body, joined and knit together by what every joint supplies, according to the effective working by which every part does its share, causes growth of the body for the edifying of itself in love" (Eph. 4:16 NKJV). Notice the phrases, "...joined and knit together by what every joint supplies," and "...causes growth of the body." Growth and edification of the body are "caused" or brought about as a result of the diverse "supplies" that come when every "joint" is "joined and knit together with the other."

This kind of "growth" goes beyond just numbers. It refers to organic, integrated growth that impacts both the physical and spiritual aspects of the body of Christ. The word "edification," derived from the Greek meaning "building," indicates spiritual development and strengthening. Such deep growth, encompassing spiritual enrichment, occurs most effectively when the unity of the body is present and strong. Such growth is seen in Acts at the start of the church. In the early church, unity not only fueled the miraculous signs and wonders of the Holy Spirit, but it also complemented them, acting as a co-catalyst and facilitator in the remarkable expansion of the church.

Unity fostered doctrinal harmony and fellowship, bringing about the blessing of growth:

> And they continued steadfastly in the apostles' doctrine and fellowship, in the breaking of bread, and in prayers. Then fear came upon every soul, and many wonders and signs were done through the apostles. Now all who believed were together, and had all things in common, and sold their possessions and goods, and divided them among all, as anyone had need.
>
> So continuing daily ***with one accord*** in the temple, and breaking bread from house to house, they ate their food with gladness and simplicity of heart, praising God and having favor with all the people. And the Lord added to the church daily those who were being saved. (Acts 2:42-47 NKJV, emphasis mine)

Unity stimulated congregational prayers that elicited powerful responses of the Holy Spirit, resulting in emboldening and strengthening against persecution:

> So, when they heard that, they raised their voice to God ***with one accord*** and said: "Lord, You are God, who made heaven and earth and the sea, and all that is in them, who by the mouth of Your servant David have said:
>
> > 'Why did the nations rage, and the people plot vain things? The kings of the earth took their stand, and the rulers were gathered together against the LORD and against His Christ.'
>
> "For truly against Your holy Servant Jesus, whom You anointed, both Herod and Pontius Pilate, with the Gentiles and the people of Israel, were gathered to do whatever Your hand and Your purpose determined before to be done. Now, Lord, look on their threats, and grant to Your servants that with all boldness they may speak Your word, by stretching out Your hand to heal, and that signs and wonders may be done through the name of Your holy Servant Jesus." And when they had prayed, the place where they were assembled together was shaken; and they were all filled with the Holy Spirit, and they spoke the word of God with boldness. (Acts 4:24-31 NKJV, emphasis mine)

Unity facilitated overcoming nationality and social

status barriers in the early church. Acts 6:1-2 states, "Now in those days, when the number of the disciples was multiplying, there arose a complaint against the Hebrews by the Hellenists, because their widows were neglected in the daily distribution." The Apostles responded to the situation by deciding to remain focused on prayer and the Word of God, while admonishing the congregation to select men to oversee the daily distribution and serving of tables. As was characteristic of the early church, "...the saying pleased the whole multitude" (Acts 6:5 NKJV), and they ***unanimously*** chose Stephen and six other men to attend to catering for the daily needs of the people. What was the result? "Then the word of God spread, and the number of the disciples multiplied greatly in Jerusalem, and a great many of the priests were obedient to the faith" (Acts 6:7 NKJV, emphasis mine).

Evidently, the early church's phenomenal growth and expansion weren't singularly because of the powerful miracles of the Holy Spirit alone, which, if not carefully managed, could lead to mainly skin-deep or superficial, numeric growth, lacking the edification and spiritual depth that are intended to take place beneath the skin, on the "joint and marrow" level. Unity accelerates and deepens the growth of the body as it functions both as a catalyst and a conduit for God's blessings to permeate the church.

A Psalmist in the Old Testament poetically depicts the dissemination of divine blessing through the instrumentality of unity:

> Behold, how good and how pleasant it is
> For brethren to dwell together in unity!
> It is like the precious oil upon the head,
> Running down on the beard,
> The beard of Aaron,
> Running down on the edge of his garments.
> It is like the dew of Hermon,
> Descending upon the mountains of Zion;
> For there the LORD commanded the blessing—
> Life forevermore. (Ps. 133 NKJV)

The vivid imagery in this Psalm powerfully illustrates how unity serves as the vital conduit through which God's blessings permeate His body. Words like "head," "running down," and "descending" are deliberately chosen to emphasize that unity is the spiritual pipeline that transmits blessings from the highest point to every member. The flow created by unity results in the entire body being touched and impacted by the anointing and refreshing from God (symbolized by the oil and the dew). Conversely, disunity acts as a barrier or shut-off valve that blocks this divine flow, preventing God's blessings from reaching His people, undermining the vitality of the body.

Not only does unity facilitate the flow of God's blessing, but it also attracts the presence of God Himself. One instance of this is evidenced in the Old Testament: the dedication of Solomon's temple. The Scripture states:

> [A]nd the Levites who were the singers, all those of Asaph and Heman and Jeduthun, with their sons and their brethren, stood at the east end of the altar, clothed in white linen, having cymbals, stringed instruments and harps, and with them one hundred and twenty priests sounding with trumpets—indeed it came to pass, when the trumpeters and singers were as one, to make one sound to be heard in praising and thanking the LORD, and when they lifted up their voice with the trumpets and cymbals and instruments of music, and praised the LORD, saying:
>
> "For He is good,
> For His mercy endures forever,"
>
> that the house, the house of the LORD, was filled with a cloud, so that the priests could not continue ministering because of the cloud; for the glory of the LORD filled the house of God (2 Chron. 5:12-14 NKJV).

The Holy Spirit vividly underscores the vital importance of unity in this extraordinary event by emphasizing the oneness of the singers and the 120 trumpeters. Notice that

God's glory descended precisely "when" they were "as one," united "to make one sound to be heard," with a single purpose – "in praising and thanking the LORD." The musicians did not think, "We, the musicians, will do our own thing while you singers sing," nor did the singers believe, "We, the vocalists, are the main focus; you, trumpeters, are just supporting." It was not "voices versus instruments" or "vocalists versus instrumentalists." No group or individual sought to outshine another. Rather, both singers and instrumentalists aligned in their minds, with their eyes fixed on an Audience of One — God — and a unified goal – praising and thanking Him. Their profound unity of mind, action, and purpose unleashed the glorious presence of God. This reveals the incredible power of unity within the body of Christ. Disunity, however, diminishes and hinders such divine outpourings, robbing the church of the fullness of God's presence and glory.

Unstoppable Together

Another reason unity is vital is that it acts as a spiritual X-factor that makes people unstoppable. When people are united, they become unstoppable and indomitable. This unique, somewhat mysterious quality of unity is confirmed in Scripture. What's more surprising is that it was during an instance when people united to oppose the will of God. Even then, unity served as the "unstoppability factor" for their plans. It was in Genesis 11, when all the people on earth spoke a single language. They agreed to go against God's creation mandate to multiply and fill the earth, and they unanimously decided to stay in one place and build the Tower of Babel, whose top would reach the sky. In other words, they united to disobey God's order:

> And they said, 'Come, let us build ourselves a city, and a tower whose top is in the heavens; let us make a name for ourselves, lest we be scattered abroad over the face of the whole earth.' But the LORD came down to see the city and the tower which the sons of men had built. And the LORD said, 'Indeed the people are one and they all have one language, and this is what they begin to do; now nothing that they propose to do will be withheld from them (Gen. 11:4-6 NKJV).

In this remarkable account of human endeavour, God's Own words show that just because of the people's unity, nothing they proposed would have failed. Although flagrantly rebellious and seemingly impossible, the Herculean task of building a tower reaching heaven was going to be achieved, all because of the X-factor of unity. This compellingly demonstrates the amazing power of unity, whether for good or ill.

This unique attribute makes unity Satan's prime target when he intends to sabotage purposes, plans, or progress. His first line of attack is disrupting the unity among people. Once accomplished, halting their progress or success immediately becomes significantly easier. In fact, to halt the rebellious Tower of Babel project, God only needed to confuse their language, and the project was doomed:

> Come, let Us go down and there confuse their language, that they may not understand one another's speech." So, the LORD scattered them abroad from there over the face of all the earth, and they ceased building the city. Therefore, its name is called Babel, because there the LORD confused the language of all the earth; and from there the LORD scattered them abroad over the face of all the earth. (Gen. 11:7-9 NKJV)

Just how many great causes have been sabotaged through the weapon of disunity? Many a relationship has been ruptured, families fractured, groups splintered, ministries devastated, and churches broken up – all as a result of disunity. Even when not totally dismantled, institutions, communities, and relationships become weakened, stagnated, or retrogressive when disunity exists. Disunity is an arrester and a stopper of progress. Underscoring the detrimental power of disunity, Jesus said, "...Every kingdom divided against itself is brought to desolation, and every city or house divided against itself will not stand" (Matt. 12:25 NKJV).

A Formidable Force

Fourthly, one of the most effective means of resisting and overcoming Satan's mischiefs against the body of Christ is operating in unity. The saying, "The whole is greater than the sum of the parts", is true when it comes to the effect of unity. For example, the Scripture reveals the potency of prayer done in unity: "Again, I say to you that if two of you agree on earth concerning anything that they ask, it will be done for them by My Father in heaven" (Matt. 18:19 NKJV). "Though one may be overpowered by another, two can withstand him. And a threefold cord is not quickly broken" (Eccles. 4:12 NKJV). Unity adds an exponential power to prayer and makes Satan no match for such spiritual offensive. The adversary can't resist a church, a people, or a family whose prayer is reinforced by unity.

A clear example of the strengthening power of unity is shown when the two greatest apostles in the Bible faced similar situations but responded very differently. Apostles Paul and Peter – both used to mistreatment and imprisonment – encountered especially difficult circumstances during their ministries in Acts 12 and Acts 16, respectively. In Acts 12, Apostle Peter was imprisoned by Herod under dire conditions. While in a dark prison, awaiting his execution, he was chained and under round-the-clock surveillance by sixteen Roman soldiers who took turns guarding his cell.

The situation was bleak and hopeless. All signs pointed to Apostle Peter suffering the same fate as Apostle James before him: execution. But God answered the church's persistent prayers and dispatched an angel to effect his supernatural rescue. However, when the angel came, he found Peter heavily asleep, a probable indication that he was overwhelmed by the circumstances and had mentally accepted his fate. He was so deeply asleep that the angel had to strike him to awaken him before leading him out of the prison.

On the other hand, Apostle Paul and his ministry partner Silas were assaulted by a mob, wrongfully arrested, beaten, and imprisoned in Philippi. However, despite these harsh treatments—bruised and battered—at midnight, with their feet in stocks in a dark, cold prison, they decided to pray and sing hymns to God. Miraculously, God responded with an earthquake that shook the prison to its foundations. Their shackles—along with those of other prisoners—were broken, and the prison doors swung open (Acts 16:16-27 NKJV). It seems that having a companion made a difference in Paul's response to his own prison ordeal, as compared to Peter's. Paul and his companions appeared to have drawn strength from each other, creating mutual inspiration amid a painful and dire situation. Had Apostle Peter had a companion as Paul did, he might have responded differently during his own imprisonment. The power of two, united, is exponential. As the popular maxim goes, there is strength in numbers—and even greater strength in unity. That fact made a difference for Paul and Silas.

Emphasis on Unity

Jesus emphasized the importance of unity in His body most strongly during His High Priestly prayer – His longest recorded prayer – found in John 17. Spanning twenty-six verses, this intercessory prayer conveys two main points: (1) Jesus' request that the Father protect the sheepfold He was about to leave from the evil one (Satan), and (2) unity within the fold. Five times in this prayer, Jesus pleads with the Father for the unity of His followers – both His immediate disciples and all who would believe in Him (verse 11, verse 21 twice, verse 22, and verse 23). If, among all Jesus could petition the Father for on behalf of His church in the final days of His earthly ministry, unity is the main concern; it clearly shows how vital unity is to the Lord Himself and His body. The sad reality, however, is that the church today does not recognize unity as being as important as Jesus did. If the Master Himself prayed so earnestly for it, then unity should be a top priority for the church.

Another strong statement on the importance of unity in the church's life was made at the very point of her inception. The New Testament church was established by the coming of the Holy Spirit in Acts 2. The account of this pivotal event in God's plan was emphatically introduced with these words, "They were all in one accord and in one place..." Why does the Holy Spirit emphasize the oneness—both physically and mentally—of the founding members during the church's beginning? Undoubtedly, to show that unity is so vital to the church that it was a necessary element for her birth to take place. The implication is that if unity was crucial for the church's birth, it is essential to her efficacious life. The question, however, is: does today's church recognize this? The answer seems to be in the negative.

Disunity - A Misdiagnosed Problem

Why disunity is not a "spirit" issue

Now, given the immense importance of unity within the body, one cannot help but ask: why then is it so difficult to be united? What causes the disunity that afflicts Christian communities, whether small or large? Answers vary depending on who you ask. Some might say the root cause is lack of love. Others would argue that human nature is responsible for disunity. However, charismatics are more likely to attribute the prevalence of disunity in the church to the "spirit of disunity" at work. In other words, we tend to believe the church suffers from demonic influences of disunity. Without question, all these factors — and others besides them — contribute to disunity in the body of Christ.

However, for those whose default response is to blame the "spirit of disunity," certain questions should be considered. What if disunity in Christ's body is not principally a "spirit" issue? What if it's not always the "spirit of disunity" that causes disunity? Could it be that the "spirit of disunity" is mostly a secondary rather than a primary cause? In other words, is it possible for disunity to exist without the presence of a "spirit of disunity"? In fact, what if the Bible reveals that the main cause of disunity in the body of Christ isn't a spirit? As surprising as it may be, the answer to all these questions is a definitive "yes".

The Bible reveals that the primary cause of disunity is the absence of something rather than merely the presence of a spirit of disunity. This idea goes against most people's assumptions, yet it holds the key to truly understanding and resolving our disunity problem. If, in fact, this is the case, then it behooves us, as believers, to conduct a thorough investigation – if truly we desire to address the issue of disunity successfully. As with any problem, the first step to finding a solution is accurate diagnosis – misdiagnosis only leads to efforts in futility. So, from this point on, we will embark on a journey to discover the vital missing element primarily responsible for disunity in the body of Christ. Buckle up, please!

A Peep under the hood – The spirit and heart

A brief analysis of man is valuable for this significant inquiry. The focus will be on the spirit, heart, and mind of man. In human makeup, the heart primarily influences the will and emotions, while the spirit serves as the conduit for receiving from and connecting with God, Who Himself is Spirit (John 4:24 NKJV). This implies that just by sharing common feelings or mutual interests on an issue, people can easily have unity at the heart level. In other words, hearts can easily align due to shared interests, goals, or similar feelings.

Similarly, agreement on the spirit level tends to be relatively easy to achieve, especially when people share the same spiritual beliefs. For example, believers who belong to the same church and are under the same spiritual or pastoral leadership are more likely to share the same spiritual beliefs and truths as they partake of the same word. They are also likely to share similar inner convictions of the Holy Spirit. Members of a local church serving in the choir, on the board of elders, in the prayer group, etc., probably do so because they share the same spiritual convictions about what they do (e.g., serving God through music, serving God through intercession for others, etc.). Essentially, certain factors can quite easily foster unity of cause (heart) and conviction (spirit). However, even in such circumstances and environments—same church, same ministry, same team, etc.—disunity, even a strong and palpable one, can still exist, and often does. The question, then, is: how is that possible? How can people's spirits and hearts be in the same place, and yet there is disunity? Where is such disunity generated or domiciled? Enter the mind.

Unity's Waterloo

The third and a powerful key player in the makeup of man is the mind. In fact, the mind plays the most significant role in the matter of unity. While the heart is the seat of man's will and feeling, the spirit is the place of inspiration and connection with God, the mind is the domain of thought and perception. The human mind can be described as the central information processing unit. What man's spirit receives from God and other spiritual sources, along with the thoughts and desires conceived within his heart, are all funneled, filtered, and processed through the mind before they are acted upon. This is why the mind ultimately determines whether there is unity or not.

The mind (the perception and information processor) is crucial in shaping our sense of unity. But unfortunately, most times, there are certain elements in the mind that are adversarial to unity, sabotaging it despite the potential for harmony within the spirit and the heart. Simply put, when it comes to unity, the human mind is where the most decisive battle is fought—more so than in the spirit or the heart. This point is vital to understand because the fate of unity largely hinges on the mind. Our actions are often driven more by our thoughts and perspectives than by our wills and feelings (i.e. our hearts) or our inspirations (i.e. our spirits). In fact, whether we are willing to accept it or not, the truth is that our minds hold greater sway over our actions than our hearts and spirits.

According to the Scripture, the human mind plays such a vital role that even after a person‘s spirit has been regenerated and his heart attuned to God, the mind remains crucial in shaping his conduct. Romans 12:2 underscores this truth: "And do not be conformed to this world, but be transformed by the renewing of your mind, that you may prove what is that good and acceptable and perfect will of God." Notice that this scripture reveals that the transformation of the believer's conduct hinges on the renewing or renovation of the mind. Recognizing this distinction between conversion and transformation of conduct is vital.

Whether a believer walks in the Spirit or the flesh largely depends on what his mind is set on: "For those who live according to the flesh set their minds on the things of the flesh, but those who live according to the Spirit, the things of the Spirit. For to be carnally minded is death, but to be spiritually minded is life and peace" (Rom. 8:5-6 NKJV). So, both the Romans 12 and Romans 8 show how significantly the believer's mind influences his spiritual life. That crucial role of the mind in the believer's life is the same reason the unity of believers is primarily controlled by the mind – not by the spirit or heart, as many assume. In matters of unity, the mind is key and king.

The Reasoning Parameters of the Mind

With the mind having so much influence over our actions notwithstanding our hearts and spirits' positions, it is apparent then that whatever dictates or directs the processes of the human mind is undeniably crucial. And that vital element is information. Besides the innate qualities of every mind, the construct of a person's mind is significantly based on, as well as influenced by the cumulated information it has been fed with or exposed to, starting from childhood. In other words, our minds are shaped by the information they absorb from our environment and experiences. This compilation of accumulated information and experiences, combined with innate knowledge, forms the framework and parameters through which our minds process data and reason thoughts.

The configuration of the mind is what is called the mindset. Simply put, a person's mindset is the lens through which his mind perceives and analyses things, and the framework it (the mind) uses in making decisions. Thoughts, ideas, or inspirations generated in the spirit or heart are channeled through the mind and are processed based on that mind's setting (the mindset), which is framed by innate and accumulated information. The mind can be likened to a computer, which uses programmed codes—sets of instructions—to analyze, evaluate, and produce outputs. The outputs from the mind constitute our actions, conduct, and behaviors.

When one becomes a Christian, his previously darkened and ignorant mind is enlightened and becomes aware of God and eternity (Eph. 4:18; 1 Cor. 4:6 NKJV). However, his mental database isn't automatically erased or overhauled. Many previously stored settings in the mind remain because much of the old data persists. This means that, after conversion, good and godly thoughts originating in the believer's spirit and heart can still be heavily influenced by pre-conversion mental configurations, leading to compromised outputs.

Consequently, for Christians, the mind remains crucial to his spirituality, as it continues to be the main processing center of their entire being.

The renewal of the mind is indispensable to the transformation of a believer's conduct. However, that renewal is a gradual process involving the removal of old information and the inculcation of new, Christ-aligned, Scripture-compliant knowledge. The accumulation of this novel knowledge gradually establishes a fresh mindset for the believer. It's important that we believers understand these crucial dynamics as it relates to our spiritual walk and growth. This means the major battleground in the Christian's spiritual walk is actually the mind. Most of the spiritual strongholds that embattle or impede spiritual progress are not in the spirit or heart chambers, but in the arena of the mind.

Unfortunately, while the believer's mind is the most besieged part of his person, it is often the most neglected asset. We often erroneously think that all we need to do is be Spirit-filled, forgetting that we must be continually mind-renewed. No matter how Spirit-filled a believer is, his mind will still process and evaluate based on its existing configurations. A significant portion of the Holy Spirit's communication with his spirit still must be channeled, analyzed, and filtered through his mind, significantly influencing his actions. Ultimately, as a Christian, your mind either supports and strengthens godly inspirations emanating from your spirit and heart or hinders them, depending on its mindset.

Egotism and Egoism

The Twin Viruses of the Mind

Egotism: Overvaluation of self-worth

Among all the processes and important evaluations our minds undertake, self-estimation or self-valuation is one of the most significant. Self-estimation predominantly occurs within our minds, and that is where the bane or boon of unity lies. Due to the impact of the Fall – Adam's fall into sin, all human minds reflect the inherent taint of sin, which significantly mars our mind's self-appraisal process. By default, our minds give us an inflated view or estimation of ourselves. A typical person thinks of himself as better or superior to others, though that thought may be unconscious. This is known as *egotism*. Formally defined, egotism is a psychological overvaluation of one's own importance or of one's own activities.[1] The root word for egotism is the Latin word *ego*, which means, *I*. That means, at the root of egotism is "I" or self.

---

[1] Alexander Moseley, "Egoism," Internet Encyclopedia of Philosophy, accessed 03/30/2026, https://iep.utm.edu/egoism

To varying degrees, most of us have the problem of egotism. The belief or feeling that "I am better than they," or "I am more important than they," unconsciously resides in the minds of most people, whether Christian or non-Christian. It might stem from spiritual gifts, physical charm, mental ability, social standing, material possessions, or personal achievements – whatever the reason, our minds subtly nurture the idea that we possess some form of superiority over others. This is the root of self-conceit or inflated self-esteem. Self-conceit is simply the overvaluation of oneself in the mind, whether one is aware of it or not. It is a flaw and affliction of the human mind.

For most people, self-conceit is more subconscious than deliberate. Usually, we aren't even aware of these mental perceptions, yet they significantly influence our actions and behaviors. As such, even when the affected person isn't aware of it or never verbally professes it, it remains tucked away in the recesses of the mind. Egotism is a mental flaw that leaves almost no one out, though it's more likely to be named only when it becomes obvious. It doesn't discriminate between old, young, new Christians, or seasoned believers. It's important that we recognize the insidious, almost ubiquitous nature of egotism. Even if you're a sincere and loving believer, there's a good chance some form of egotism—the elevated "I" and "self'—still secretly resides in your mind.

When our minds suggest we are better than others and we consent to that notion – whether consciously or unconsciously – maintaining unity with others becomes inevitably more difficult, even with those who share our thoughts and beliefs. Because of the "superiority" mentality rooted in egotism, when others' ideas or opinions don't align with ours, we naturally assume they are the ones in the wrong. And since we already see ourselves as superior, yielding or deferring our own opinions is usually not an option. As such, when conflicts arise from differences of opinion, though we believe in the same purposes and perhaps even the same goals, it doesn't take much for us to disagree, disunite or disconnect from others – after all, the "lesser" is in need of the "greater," not the other way around.

The Bible recounts a grave case of egotism that ultimately led to the downfall of a man renowned for his wisdom and influence – Ahitophel. Ahitophel appeared to have been the foremost royal adviser to King David. His advice was so highly valued that it was described in superlatives: "Now the advice of Ahithophel, which he gave in those days, was as if one had inquired at the oracle of God. So was all the advice of Ahithophel both with David and with Absalom" (2 Sam. 16:23 NKJV). However, Ahitophel suffered from the virus of egotism. According to the Scriptures, when the self-appointed king, Absalom, asked for guidance on how to pursue and overthrow his exiled father, David, who was fleeing, Ahithophel offered counsel that was perfectly tactical and logical. Yet, to Ahitophel's shock - and perhaps unprecedented - another adviser's counsel was accepted instead. Absalom chose to follow Hushai's words. The sage's reaction exposed his deep-seated ego issue. The wise man could not accept the rejection of his advice. The denial was utterly intolerable for him. He resorted to the ultimate remedy – suicide:

> Now, when Ahithophel saw that his advice was not followed, he saddled a donkey and arose and went home to his house, to his city. Then he put his household in order, and hanged himself, and died; and he was buried in his father's tomb. (2 Sam. 17:23 NKJV)

It's the ego factor. Ahitophel believed he was the best counsellor. Nobody could give better advice than his. He was so full of himself that he could not stomach rejection, especially a royal one. He would rather die than be rejected or deemed inferior in his counsel – even for once. Although he was indeed a wise man, he was plagued with an acute problem of egotism.

Like Ahitophel, inflated self-valuation leads people to believe that others need them more than they need others. It makes them feel that getting along with others is not really necessary. When egotism is at play, we often believe that our association with others benefits them more than it benefits us. We feel that the need for belonging is mostly others'. As a result, if things fail, they will be the ones to lose our contributions to their lives, but not necessarily the other way around. Such a mindset makes maintaining unity with others neither necessary nor a priority. This is the mindset—whether conscious or unconscious—that underpins the behavior of many people who find it hard to sustain cohesive relationships. That difficulty in sustaining relationships is driven by an inflated valuation of oneself in the mind. It doesn't necessarily mean that such a person has a resentful heart towards others, or a bad spirit, or that he or she is not a true follower of Christ. The issue isn't necessarily a "spirit" problem or a "heart" problem. It's a mindset issue. It's egotism.

So, if you ever wondered why some good-hearted, Spirit-filled Christians struggle to maintain the "spirit of unity" with others, egotism is often a key factor. If you have ever been puzzled by the inability of some respected and admired spiritual leaders to get along with each other, or questioned why churches and ministries split over minor, reconcilable issues, egotism is a major cause. When you are a talented, Spirit-filled church worker but find it difficult to get along with fellow ministers or co-church workers, it's likely due to an overestimation of your own importance. If you're a minister of the gospel and maintaining harmony with other ministers seems challenging, it's time to check your ego – egotism is almost certainly involved. No matter your position, power, or privileges, if you struggle to keep unity with other believers—except when serious doctrinal differences are involved—the first thing to examine is your ego. An inflated self-image or sense of self-importance might be taking hold of your mind. You may not be fully aware of it, but some level of superiority complex most likely exists deep within. It's essential to uncover and address it. Ask yourself, "How do I truly rate or appraise myself in relation to others?" "Do I perceive myself as more significant or important than they?"

Egoism: Prioritization of self-interest

Egoism or selfish ambition is also a flaw of the mind. Notice the difference between the two words: egotism versus egoism. While egotism is elevated self-valuation, egoism refers to heightened ambition – specifically selfish ambition. It is the promotion and preoccupation with self-interest. It also resides within the mind. Naturally, somewhere in the back of our minds, we tend to rationalize and convince ourselves that our own matters are more important than others'. We are inclined to believe that our needs and desires, as well as the realization of both, matter more than those of others. Like egotism, egoism rarely spares anyone; it can secretly nestle in almost anyone's mind. It's a widespread mental bug. It also represents a delinquency in "I" or "self" estimation. Therefore, both egotism and egoism are viruses that tend to burrow deep into the minds of both the best and the rest of us.

When selfish ambition—placing one's own benefit and gain above all else— takes hold, it rapidly undermines shared goals and collective well-being. This mindset ultimately eclipses any genuine kindness or integrity that is brought to a relationship or cause. Egoism whispers, "I deserve this," "I need to have this," "this must serve my purposes or else," "my satisfaction outweighs everything." Whether driven by the desire for recognition, praise, status, power, control, or financial gain, such a perspective almost always sparks conflicts of interest. It relentlessly tears apart unity and trust, making collaboration impossible.

Perhaps a good question to ask at this point is: what attitude would you say describes the prevailing mindset in your relationship and dealings within your family - with your spouse, your children, or siblings? Is it "what works for me," or "what works for us"? Are the decisions in your group, team, or ministry tailored to what benefits you or what benefits "us"? Are you more concerned about how you feel or about how "we" feel? When and where the answers to these questions go with personal rather than plural pronouns, unity is typically scarce or tenuous.

King Solomon underscores egoism as a divider and separator of people: "A man who isolates himself seeks his own desire; he rages against all wise judgment" (Prov. 18:1 NKJV). This Scripture emphasizes that at times, the true cause of mysterious separation or isolation of individuals from a family, group, team, ministry, or church is none other than egoism. Such separations are often driven by a pursuit of personal, selfish desires. The reality of this Scripture is widely attested to in factions and breakaways seen in churches and Christian ministries across the world today.

Most of the devastating breakups within these sacred institutions are caused by individuals driven by selfish ambition. Many such breakups begin with disunity between one or more individuals and the rest of the group, which might be hard to notice at first. It then develops into more open discontent, ultimately leading to a complete breakup. The truth is that, for the most part, instigators and leaders of factionalism and sedition within the body of Christ are simply individuals who "seek [their] own desire." They are individuals overtaken by egoism. It should not be surprising if it's found that many breakaway leaders of churches or ministries make little or no changes in their new groups, except in areas that give them unfettered access to personal interests they have always cherished but were unable to fulfil in their previous settings.

While ruptures and fragmentations within the body of believers reveal the destructive power of egoism or selfish ambition, family and personal relationships are not immune to its effects. Egoism weakens personal relationships and separates family members. If you're struggling to get along with your spouse or another family member, you should consider whether selfish ambition is at play. Tense or conflict-ridden relationships with ministerial or departmental brethren, coworkers, business partners, and others also likely indicate the presence of egoism somewhere. Whenever someone constantly wants everything or every outcome to favor him, or has a "I win, or nobody wins" mentality, it's a clear sign of egoism, and maintaining friendly, healthy long-term relationships becomes difficult. Where egoism exists, conflicts are inevitable, and unity is hard to maintain.

Since, by nature, unity involves aligning oneself in agreement with others, egotism and egoism are its two biggest enemies. This implies that achieving unity is impossible without addressing egotism and egoism. It's no surprise then that when it comes to believers' unity, more than ten Scriptures reference the mind, since this is where the "ego" issues emanate from: Rom. 12:16; 15:5-6; 1 Cor. 1:10; 2 Cor. 13:11; Phil. 1:27; 2:1-5; 3:16; 4:2; 1 Pet. 3:8; Rev. 17:17 NKJV). Disunity is fundamentally a "mind" issue, not a "spirit" issue.

The Blueprint to Unity

Apostolic Wisdom for a United Church

Among the many Scriptures that call for unity, Apostle Paul's letter to the Philippians stands out. In the second chapter of his letter, Apostle Paul reveals that the solution to the problem of disunity within the body of Christ involves two steps: 1) removing anti-unity mindsets; and 2) cultivating a mindset that encourages unity.

Let's take an in-depth look at Philippians 2:1-6 NKJV:

> Therefore, if there is any consolation in Christ, if any comfort of love, if any fellowship of the Spirit, if any affection and mercy, fulfill my joy by being like-minded, having the same love, being of one accord, of one mind. Let nothing be done through selfish ambition or conceit, but in lowliness of mind let each esteem others better than himself. Let each of you look out not only for his own interests, but also for the interests of others. Let this mind be in you which was also in Christ Jesus, who, being in the form of God, did not consider it robbery to be equal with God, but made Himself of no

> reputation, taking the form of a bondservant, and coming in the likeness of men. And being found in appearance as a man, He humbled Himself and became obedient to the point of death, even the death of the cross. Therefore God also has highly exalted Him and given Him the name which is above every name, that at the name of Jesus every knee should bow, of those in heaven, and of those on earth, and of those under the earth, and that every tongue should confess that Jesus Christ is Lord, to the glory of God the Father.

Context

It appears the members of the church in Philippi were missing out on the communal spiritual benefits of being part of the body of Christ. These benefits include the comfort of love (the reassurance that brotherly love provides), the fellowship of the Spirit (the communion of the Holy Spirit), and brotherly affection and mercy – all of which members of Christ's body should experience and enjoy. The absence of these benefits seems to have stemmed from lack of unity among the Philippian Christians. The apostle now urges them towards unity, explaining that seeing them come together, experience, and enjoy these collective spiritual blessings would bring him great joy. To achieve this, Paul offers apostolic guidance on fostering that essential unity. He begins with a negative instruction — what not to do — and immediately follows with a positive one — what to do.

The negative command is: “Let nothing be done through selfish ambition or conceit” (verse 3a). Here, the apostle’s first instruction proscribes egoism and egotism, using selfish ambition and conceit as synonyms for the two terms – selfish ambition for egoism, and conceit signifies egotism, respectively.

Get Rid of Egoism

According to Apostle Paul’s instructions, the first step in overcoming disunity is to eliminate egoism. He advises, “Let nothing be done through selfish ambition or conceit” (Phil. 2:3a NKJV). This reveals that, for unity to be achieved within the church of God—and in other relationships, too—selfish ambition, or egoism, must be addressed first. Personal benefits must not be the sole motivation in any relationships where unity is desired. As Christians, we need to train our minds to recognize that when in any relationship, our interests should not be the only “legitimate” or “important’ ones; rather, the benefits and interests of others should be valued and pursued as well. Put simply, if "what’s in it for me?” or “how will this benefit me?” dominates your thoughts when making decisions or responding to issues, it will be difficult to build genuine unity with others. Whether in marriage, friendships, or within a group or community, selfish ambition must be discarded in all that the believer does. Regardless of your status or role, your primary focus should not be “me,” “myself,” and “I.” As a believer, you must consciously and actively fight against selfish ambition—both in thoughts and actions. This is part 1 of

Apostle Paul's "how-to" guide on achieving unity. Without this initial step, unity might remain only a wish.

Get rid of Egotism (Self-conceit)

Part b of the first step to unity is to eliminate egotism (self-conceit) - the second mind-enemy of unity: "Let nothing be done through selfish ambition or conceit" (verse 3a). It is hard to be united with those you believe you are better than or superior to. When such associations exist, they are usually fragile, maintained only on your own terms. Romans 12:16 says, "Be of the same mind toward one another. Do not set your mind on high things, but associate with the humble. Do not be wise in your own opinion." High-mindedness breeds disunity.

So, biblical apostolic wisdom demands that both egoism and egotism be first addressed and eliminated from the minds of believers who intend to experience unity in the church, ministry, community, or family.

Elimination by Substitution

However, knowing what to eliminate doesn't necessarily mean knowing how to do so. So, how do we rid our minds of these two enemies of unity? It's through elimination by substitution. Egoism and egotism must be replaced with two contrasting mental attitudes. In other words, achieving unity is more than just about removing certain things; it's about replacing them with new qualities. This process involves a mental transformation in which the old way of thinking is replaced with a new one. Let's take a look again at Apostle Paul's carefully structured injunction to the Philippians involving deconstruction and reconstruction:

A) "Let nothing be done with selfish ambition [egoism] or conceit [egotism]" (Phil. 2:3a NKJV, emphasis mine).
B) But in lowliness of mind, let each esteem others better than himself. Let each of you look out not only for his own interests, but also for the interests of others (Phil. 2:3b-4 NKJV, emphasis mine)

Observe how "Let not..." in the first statement is followed by "Let..." in the second. The mental virtues outlined in the second statement are the antidotes to the mental faults censured in the first. In other words, egoism and egotism must be eliminated, while humility and selflessness should be cultivated. This mental transformation is crucial for attaining unity within the body of Christ.

Another key observation is that the injunction, "Let each esteem others better than himself," is introduced by the phrase "In lowliness of mind." This qualifier is significant because it reveals that valuing others above oneself is fundamentally a characteristic of the mind—specifically, a humble and lowly mind. This same qualifier also applies to the second behavior prescribed, "looking out for others' interests." Essentially, the use of the qualifier "in lowliness of mind" means that just as egotism and egoism are rooted in the mind, so too are humility and selflessness mind-based characteristics.

Further confirming that humility and selflessness are mental attitudes is the injunction in the very next verse: "Let this mind be in you which was also in Christ," (verse 5). This again identifies the two aforementioned qualities, humility and selflessness, as attributes of the mind. They are specifically qualities of the mind of Christ. The key conclusion from these observations is that unity is primarily a matter of the mind; therefore, transforming the mind is key to achieving it. To achieve unity, as Christians, our minds must undergo deconstruction and reconstruction. When the egocentric mindset is dismantled and the mind of Christ is cultivated, unity will spread throughout the body of Christ.

A Deeper Look

Given the assertions so far, perhaps a valid question to ask at this point is: do Christians not already possess the mind of Christ? Should true believers be told to "let the mind of Christ" be in them? These are pertinent and, in fact, crucial questions that demand serious consideration. They address an important topic that should not be overlooked.

Firstly, every genuine Christian is indwelt by the Spirit of God—without this, one cannot truly be a Christian. As Romans 8:9 states, "But you are not in the flesh but in the Spirit, if indeed the Spirit of God dwells in you. Now if anyone does not have the Spirit of Christ, he is not His"

(NKJV). Similarly, Galatians 4:6 affirms, "And because you are sons, God has sent forth the Spirit of His Son into your hearts, crying out, "Abba, Father!"' At salvation, God's Holy Spirit is immediately given to every believer. In his epistle to the Corinthian church, Apostle Paul writes: "Therefore I make known to you that no one speaking by the Spirit of God calls Jesus accursed, and no one can say that Jesus is Lord except by the Holy Spirit" (1 Cor. 12:3 NKJV). While this is distinct from the baptism of the Holy Spirit, the indwelling of the Holy Spirit is an unwavering mark of authentic Christianity. It is essential to understand that without this indwelling, genuine faith simply cannot exist.

However, there is a significant difference between having the Spirit of Christ and possessing the mind of Christ. Primarily, the Spirit of Christ is received, whereas the mind of Christ is developed. Every Christian has the Spirit of Christ (the Holy Spirit), but not every Christian has cultivated the mind of Christ. Additionally, the spirit pertains to "being (who we are)," while the mind relates to "knowing (awareness of) who we are." Often, a significant gap exists between the new creation we became in our spirit-man at conversion and how much we understand about this new creation. This is where the disparity between the *person* of the new creation and the *practice* of the new creature emerges. Most of the discrepancies stem from our limited understanding of our true identity as a new creation in the spirit-man. Beyond that, discrepancies also emerge from our mentality—the way we think—which also partly stems from a limited perception of our new self-identity.

The conformity of the believer's mind to the Spirit of Christ in him is not automatic. Although the believer has the Spirit of Christ, he still has to bring his mind into harmony with that Spirit within. This is a process that involves the believer's active participation. Consequently, it is entirely possible to be a Christian indwelt by the Spirit yet still have the mind of Christ not fully developed or not developed at all. Every Christian must choose whether to align his mind with Christ or to conform it to the dispositions of the flesh. This is why the Apostle Paul, in his letter to the Romans, writes, "And do not be conformed to this world, but be transformed by the renewing of your mind, that you may prove what is that good and acceptable and perfect will of God." Conversion and conformity are two different events.

An incident involving Jesus's 12 disciples, especially James and John, highlights the difference between conversion and conformity of mind. On one occasion, Jesus was refused permission to pass through Samaria to Jerusalem. James and John were not at all shy about making their displeasure known. In fact, beyond that, they were ready to see the Samaritans decimated right away.

> Now it came to pass, when the time had come for Him to be received up, that He steadfastly set His face to go to Jerusalem, and sent messengers

> before His face. And as they went, they entered a village of the Samaritans, to prepare for Him. But they did not receive Him, because His face was set for the journey to Jerusalem. And when His disciples James and John saw this, they said, "Lord, do You want us to command fire to come down from heaven and consume them, just as Elijah did?" But He turned and rebuked them, and said, "You do not know what manner of spirit you are of. For the Son of Man did not come to destroy men's lives but to save them." And they went to another village. (Luke 9:51-56 NKJV).

What do we see here? We find two of Jesus's disciples about to respond to a situation in a way that was completely out of line with what Jesus would have expected of His followers. Jesus sharply rebuked them for their incorrect, unloving response. However, beyond just a mere disapproval, the content of Jesus' rebuke reveals an important spiritual truth. Jesus said, "You do not know what manner of spirit you are of." Jesus' statement reveals that the issue was not the absence of the Spirit of grace in these two disciples; rather, it was their ignorance of the character of the Spirit of Christ within them – and that ignorance shaped their course of action. Though they were believers and disciples of the Lord, John and James neither knew the nature of the Spirit with them nor had they developed the mind of Christ.

However, years later, the contrast between the John on that occasion and the John who, authored the Epistles of John - the books that speak about love more than any other in the entire Bible – is unmistakable. By the time he penned the Epistles, John had become the "apostle of love," the complete opposite of the "let fire fall and burn them up" personality he once was. So, although the Spirit was always within him, it took a while for his mind to be shaped and to align with the Spirit of Christ in him.

But it was not just James and John who had times of acting contrary to the Spirit of grace to Whom they belonged; the entire cadre of disciples exhibited the same contradiction between their spirit and their mind. Just before the story of John and James, the disciples were engaged in a dispute over who would be the greatest among them. Here is that pericope from the book of Mark:

> Then He came to Capernaum. And when He was in the house He asked them, "What was it you disputed among yourselves on the road?" But they kept silent, for on the road they had disputed among themselves who would be the greatest. And He sat down, called the twelve, and said to them, "If anyone

> desires to be first, he shall be last of all and servant of all." Then He took a little child and set him in the midst of them. And when He had taken him in His arms, He said to them, "Whoever receives one of these little children in My name receives Me; and whoever receives Me, receives not Me but Him who sent Me. (Mark 9:33-37 NKJV)

Right here, egotism was glaringly evident among Jesus' disciples. "I will be the greatest," "no, you won't," "I am the oldest," "I am the most loved," "I have the greatest faith"—the arguments continued. What was the outcome of such an egotistic exchange? Dispute and, of course, disunity— "for on the road they had disputed among themselves..." Remarkably, according to Luke's account, this was after their successful mission in which they cast out demons and healed the sick. Yet, afterwards, they argued over who would be the greatest. It's clear that their problem wasn't spiritual but mental; it was an egotistical mindset issue. The display of power and miracles may have even fueled their pride and contention. Not much has changed today. Often, Christians, including ministers of God, not only fail to unite but also get involved in disputes and fights. It's mainly egotism of the mind at work, even though the Holy Spirit dwells within. Recognizing these spirit versus mind dynamics is essential to arresting disunity in the body of Christ.

Now, back to Apostle Paul's statement in Philippians 2. Given the often significant gap between the spirit and the mind of the Christian, Apostle Paul's admonition of the Philippian believers to "let" the mind of Christ dwell in them is perfectly legitimate. This act of "letting" is, in fact, a matter of necessity at all stages of spiritual maturity—from new converts to seasoned saints. In other words, deliberateness is required when it comes to aligning the believer's mind with the wills and ways of the Holy Spirit within. As a result, the mental attitudes of humility and selflessness required to forge and foster unity with others might not come to the believer automatically or naturally. That means the believer must often intentionally and actively choose to cultivate Christ's humble, selfless mindset, deliberately rejecting egocentric, flesh-driven attitudes that hinder true unity.

Another important point is that the conformity of a believer's mind to the Holy Spirit occurs in degrees. A believer's submission to the Holy Spirit in certain aspects of his life does not necessarily mean that submission in all aspects of his thoughts, conduct, or behavior has already taken place. The truth is that, more often than not, there are pockets and portions of the believer's thoughts and mindset that are yet to align with Christ's nature. Conformity to Christ's mind is not a one-off event; it is a gradual, ongoing process. The implication of this is that unity may be difficult to achieve among Christians whose minds still harbor egoism and egotism, in whom the humble and selfless qualities of Christ's mind are yet to be developed – despite significant development in other areas.

Taking a moment for personal reflection, would you say you have truly addressed and overcome egoism and egotism within your mind? Have you cultivated humility and other-mindedness, which are qualities of Christ's mind and prerequisites for unity?

Christ's Mind Under the Microscope

The art of humility and selflessness

How do we develop this mindset?

An all-important question at this point is: how do we actually go about developing these two attributes of Christ's mind – humility and selflessness? As with most things in life, there are always exceptions to the rule. There are individuals whom God engraces such that humility and selflessness come almost naturally to them – whether as Christians or even before they become Christians. But in truth, these cases are few and far between. For most believers, humility and selflessness are qualities that only emerge after some spiritual shaping and growth. They are virtues usually nurtured through deliberate effort, prayer, and practice. That means if they haven't come naturally for you, you are in the majority. There is hope.

Practicing Humility

What does practicing humility look like? The anchor scripture, Philippians 2:3, holds the answer. Verse 3b reads, "...in lowliness of mind, let each esteem the other better than himself.' This verse describes humility as self-abasement—lowering oneself. True practice of humility involves self-lowering and esteeming of others as "better than" oneself. This esteeming of others as better does not mean that "the other" is actually more important, but rather, it means you consider or reckon him as if he is. In other words, it's a deliberate act of lowering oneself so as to honor another, regardless of one's true status. Another verse expresses this as, "... in honor, giving preference to one another" (Rom. 12:10 NKJV). Essentially, humility isn't about only honoring someone of a higher status; it's about willingly setting aside one's own importance or status and giving honor to all, including those of lower status. Apostle Peter underscores this in 1 Peter 2:17: "Honor all people. Love the brotherhood. Fear God. Honor the king" (NKJV).

The ultimate example of true humility is our Lord Jesus Himself. The greatest expression of self-abasement was displayed in our Lord, Jesus Christ's coming into the world. Before His incarnation, Jesus shared essence, form, as well as glory with the Father— "Who, being in the form of God, did not consider it robbery to be equal with God..." (Phil. 2:6a NKJV). The fact of Jesus' existence in the same glory with the Father was attested to by the Lord Himself in His High Priestly prayer: "And now, O Father, glorify Me together with Yourself, with the glory which I had with You before the world was" (John 17:5 NKJV). Notice the last phrase— "...the glory which I had with You before the world was." Prophet Isaiah testified to this when he saw the preincarnate Jesus in His glory as the exalted LORD of hosts, worshipped by the seraphim, and Whose glory filled the whole earth..

> In the year that King Uzziah died, I saw the sitting on a throne, high and lifted In the year that King Uzziah died, I saw the Lord sitting on a throne, high and lifted up, and the train of His robe filled the temple. Above it stood seraphim; each one had six wings: with two he covered his face, with two he covered his feet, and with two he flew. And one cried to another and said:
> "Holy, holy, holy is the LORD of hosts;
> The whole earth is full of His glory!"
> And the posts of the door were shaken by the voice of him who cried out, and the house was filled with smoke. (Isa. 6:1-4 NKJV)

However, the incredible and incomprehensible happened at the incarnation. The glorious King and LORD of Hosts decided to step down from His exalted throne, set aside His glory and majesty, divest Himself of His divine "form of God" and "equality with God", and take on a mortal body of clay, descending to earth as a baby through the womb of a teenage girl. What could be more unimaginable? The One by Whom, through Whom, and for Whom all things were created, One Who is so high that He "humbles Himself to behold the things that are in the heavens and in the earth" (Col. 1:16); Ps. 113:6 NKJV), lowered Himself so much that He became as one of His own creations. So undignified was His entry into the world that He was born where no baby would have consented to be born – at the feeding trough of animals. In the greatest act of humility, Jesus divested Himself of indescribable glory and became an inhabitant of this sin-stained, sordid earth. He "made Himself of no reputation, taking the form of a bondservant, and coming in the likeness of men. And being found in appearance as a man, He humbled Himself and became obedient to the point of death, even the death of the cross" (Phil. 2:7-8 NKJV).

But while Jesus' humility surpasses anything imaginable by humans, what makes it even more remarkable is that it was not coerced or demanded by the Father. It was entirely self-imposed; voluntary. Jesus, of His own accord, humbled Himself, not because the Father required or mandated it. Notice Philippians 2:7 says, "made Himself of no reputation." Jesus' emptying Himself of His glory was a completely free will act. In His own words, Jesus said, "Therefore My Father loves Me, because I lay down My life that I may take it again. No one takes it from Me, but I lay it down of Myself. I have power to lay it down, and I have power to take it again. This command I have received from My Father" (John 10:17-18 NKJV). By all accounts, Jesus' self-abasement to come to serve and save mortal men is the height of esteeming "others better than oneself." That is why the Apostle Paul called humility the "mind of Christ." This mindset is the basis of true humility. Self-abasement is the ultimate neutralizer of egotism. It is therefore the mindset that must be in place for genuine unity to thrive, as without true humility, it's difficult for unity to subsist.

Remember the disciples of Jesus who were egotistically debating who was the greatest among them? Well, they also later showed how, even during a fierce argument, humility could still bring about unity. As recorded in Acts 15, in the early days of the church, some Jewish Christians believed that Christians still needed to be circumcised. They went around preaching circumcision requirement to the brethren, contradicting Apostle Paul's teachings. When the issue could no longer be contained or ignored, Apostle Paul decided to bring it to the Jerusalem Council, made up of the Apostles and elders of the church. However, it proved to be a sensitive and divisive matter even for the congregation in Jerusalem.

When the debate grew heated, Apostle Peter stood up to address the congregation, reminding them how God had sent him years earlier to take the gospel to the uncircumcised Gentiles. He stated that since God did not require it, there was no need to burden the Gentile believers with the requirement of circumcision. Another Apostle, James, also addressed the assembly, affirming Peter's position on the matter. After the Apostles' speeches and the testimonies of Paul and Barnabas, the conference reached a decision that serves as a classic example of how, amid divisive and contentious issues, unity can still prevail within the body of Christ. Below is the joint statement issued by the body:

> The apostles, the elders, and the brethren, To the brethren who are of the Gentiles in Antioch, Syria, and Cilicia:
>
> Greetings.
>
> Since we have heard that some who went out from us have troubled you with words, unsettling your souls, saying, "You must be circumcised and keep the law"—to whom we gave no such commandment— it seemed good to us, being assembled with one accord, to send chosen men to you with our beloved Barnabas and Paul, men who have risked their lives for the name of our Lord Jesus Christ. We have therefore sent Judas and Silas, who will also report the same things by word of mouth. For it seemed good to the Holy Spirit, and to us, to lay upon you no greater burden than these necessary things: that you abstain from things offered to idols, from blood, from things strangled, and from sexual immorality. If you keep yourselves from these, you will do well. Farewell. (Acts 15:23-29 NKJV)

How did the assembly manage to reach this unanimous decision? The "how" is where the lesson in unity is for us. Firstly, the leading apostles, Peter and James – especially Peter, who had firsthand knowledge and experience on the circumcision issue and could be braggadocious about it, should they choose to – approached the situation with humility rather than an authoritative tone. They did not preempt the decision, but rather allowed those with differing opinions to weigh in. This is a lesson for church leaders. On the other hand, some in leadership who held different views were also willing to relinquish their positions and agree with the leading apostles – demonstrating submission. The result of these choices was the coming together and resolution of a touchy matter.

Notice the unmistakable unity in their resolution despite such a challenging and contentious debate: "it seemed good to us, being assembled with one accord..." Such unity was only possible through humility and a willingness to yield. It exemplifies the words of Ephesians 4:3: "... endeavoring to keep the unity of the Spirit in the bond of peace." Whereas conflict previously arose from the disciples' egotistical mindset, when later faced with a situation that could have torn the church apart, unity and peaceful resolution flourished because of humility.

Again, looking inward, perhaps you have noticed self-exalting or self-glorifying tendencies or thoughts in the corridors of your mind. Maybe you find it hard to show humility towards others. A practical step is to start esteeming and honoring others as if they are greater than you—even when you know they are not. Begin thinking less of your status, position, power, importance, or greatness. With intentionality and prayer, you can cultivate a self-abasing mindset—Christ's mindset. This may manifest by way of yielding to others, giving precedence to others, verbally honoring others, deliberately lowering yourself to the level of others, or refusing to be preoccupied with or overly attached to certain rights and privileges.

`Imagine the kind of atmosphere that would be enjoyed in churches, ministries, men's groups, women's groups, volunteer groups, and families, if everyone were to esteem and honor the other as if he or she were better than himself or herself. How welcoming and edifying would the atmosphere be where "I am this," "I am that," "who is he?" or "who is she?" attitudes have no place in anyone's mind! It would be an egotism-free zone, where unity of brethren is easily achieved and sustained. Such an environment can be created almost in every home, church, and community if only believers would develop the mind of Christ – a humble mind. Desiring unity means we must be ready to adopt this self-abasing mentality. It must be our way of thinking and relating to others.

So, how do you see yourself in relation to others – as superior to them or in humble esteem? Do you give deference and preference to others, or do you typically consider yourself more important or better than others?

Practicing Other-mindedness

The second attribute of Christ's mind needed for unity is other-mindedness, or simply, selflessness. "Let each of you look out not only for his own interests, but also for the interests of others" (Phil. 2:4 NKJV). Like self-abasement (humility), there is no greater example of this than our Lord Himself. Jesus left His glory and came to earth because He considered our plight. He was mindful of us. He came, not because He had a need, but because we had a need. He was not self-minded, but us-minded. When the Scripture says, Jesus "did not consider it robbery to be equal with God," the word "robbery" is the English translation of the Greek word *harpagmos*, which means "a thing to be seized upon or held fast, retained." It means Jesus, because of man's needs, did not consider His equality in essence and glory with God something to be held unto. If Jesus had been only minded of His glory, no way would He have left the majesty of His glorious, exalted throne to be clothed with a mortal body.

It was his immense, selfless love for humanity that made the degradation and pain of the incarnation of the Lord bearable. The thrice-holy God, Who knew no sin, had to become sin in the process of saving us: "For He made Him who knew no sin to be sin for us, that we might become the righteousness of God in Him" (2 Cor. 5:21 NKJV). The One into whose eyes no created being ever gazed was spat upon and slapped in the face by mere mortals (John 18:22). The judge of heaven and earth became the accused, was arraigned, and condemned alongside criminals. The One Who Himself is life was made to taste death, laid in the dust, and covered with the earth.

What in the world could have motivated such a sacrifice? Why did the King of Glory go through all this? It was selfless love and concern for mankind. Jesus had man's best interests at heart. Though He did not need us to add anything to Him, yet He gave up His glory, honor, and splendor. This is the reason why prioritizing others' interests is a Christlike mindset. Such a mentality neutrializes self-centeredness that impedes unity. For unity to thrive, other-mindedness must be cultivated. Intentionally thinking about the well-being of others and voluntarily sacrificing our rights, preferences, and convenience for it are practical ways to cultivate this mindset.

Apostle Paul was also an example of an other-minded, egoism-free believer. Though he was a Jew, his selflessness enabled him to effectively reach and serve people from various backgrounds, races, and beliefs. In his own words, the apostle wrote:

> For though I am free from all men, I have made myself a servant to all, that I might win the more; and to the Jews I became as a Jew, that I might win Jews; to those who are under the law, as under the law, that I might win those who are under the law; to those who are

> without law, as without law (not being without law toward God, but under law toward Christ), that I might win those who are without law; to the weak I became as weak, that I might win the weak. I have become all things to all men, that I might by all means save some. Now this I do for the gospel's sake, that I may be partaker of it with you. (1 Cor. 9:19-23 NKJV)

Notice Apostle Paul's decision to make "myself a servant to all," so that he might "win the more." He became "all things to all men," that "I might by all means save some." Clearly, Paul's approach to life and ministry was not "what's in it for me?" It wasn't, "How can this serve my purpose?" Instead of prioritizing his own interests in ministry, Apostle Paul's mentality was to seek the good of as many people as possible, even if that meant sacrificing, adapting, and giving up his personal preferences – so long as others were reached and brought to Christ. What a great mindset! It's the very opposite of "I, me, and myself," "my way or no way" egoistic mentality. No wonder he was so versatile in his usefulness to the Lord.

When we pursue and practice pleasing others, unity becomes easier to achieve and maintain, as things will not always need to go our way. Decisions will no longer have to be made to our own advantage, at the expense of others.

We won't need to agree with every group decision before supporting it. Yielding our preferences for the benefit of others will become simpler.

If you aim to be a unity-seeker, you must develop the mindset that the family, group, team, or ministry you are part of isn't primarily about what you can gain. Instead, whatever community you are part of should benefit everyone involved. To adopt this way of thinking, for example, you might ask yourself: what changes or adjustments could I make within my home just because they would help others in my family—my husband, wife, or children—even if the current situation benefits me more? Community-wise, how much better would your group or ministry be if, even when a decision doesn't necessarily align with you or another member, everyone still gives his or her best effort and support?

Imagine that in your group, everyone is okay with times when his or her ideas or suggestions are not taken or are overridden by others in the interest of the group, without any bad feelings or gossip. These scenarios are all real possibilities and reflect the ideals of the body of Christ when selflessness is embraced and practiced. Blessed is the church, group, team, or family where such a spirit and atmosphere exist. True unity will flourish in such places because personal egos are set aside, no one needs to be the center of attention, and life does not revolve around any individual's self-interest. Such a place is where egoism gives way to selflessness.

As has been propounded and demonstrated, disunity in the church mainly stems from believers' mindsets, and less from a spirit of disunity, although the latter can sometimes be a real culprit. The Scripture clearly shows the mental transformation that must happen for unity to thrive in churches, ministries, communities, and families. The twin mental viruses of egotism and egoism must be eradicated and replaced with the attributes of humility and other-mindedness of Christ's mind. Since most people are affected by ego issues, nearly every Christian—regardless of spiritual maturity—needs to make this mental transformation. Given that unity is vital for the church to experience the full blessings the Father desires for and has bestowed upon the body of Christ, these mental changes are crucial. Misdiagnosing the cause of disunity is one reason it has remained a nemesis for the church. By cultivating the mind of Christ, unity can become a reality within His body. The question is: would you allow the change to start with you, your family, your group, and your church?

Appendix

More Scriptures on unity:

Revelation 17:17
For God has put it into their hearts to fulfill His purpose, to be of one mind, and to give their kingdom to the beast, until the words of God are fulfilled.

1 Peter 3:8
Finally, all of you be of one mind, having compassion for one another; love as brothers, be tenderhearted, be courteous;

Philippians 4:2
I implore Euodia and I implore Syntyche to be of the same mind in the Lord.

Philippians 3:16
Nevertheless, to the degree that we have already attained, let us walk by the same rule, let us be of the same mind.

Philippians 2:1-2
Therefore if there is any consolation in Christ, if any comfort of love, if any fellowship of the Spirit, if any affection and mercy, [2] fulfill my joy by being like-minded, having the same love, being of one accord, of one mind

Philippians 1:27
27 Only let your conduct be worthy of the gospel of Christ,
so that whether I come and see you or am absent, I may
hear of your affairs, that you stand fast in one spirit, with
one mind striving together for the faith of the gospel,

2 Corinthians 13:11
11 Finally, brethren, farewell. Become complete. Be of
good comfort, be of one mind, live in peace; and the God
of love and peace will be with you.

1 Corinthians 1:10
10 Now I plead with you, brethren, by the name of our
Lord Jesus Christ, that you all speak the same thing, and
that there be no divisions among you, but that you be
perfectly joined together in the same mind and in the
same judgment.

Romans 15:5-6
Now may the God of patience and comfort grant you to
be like-minded toward one another, according to Christ
Jesus, 6 that you may with one mind and one mouth
glorify the God and Father of our Lord Jesus Christ.

Romans 12:16
16 Be of the same mind toward one another. Do not set
your mind on high things, but associate with the humble.
Do not be wise in your own opinion.